THE
MOON

TIM FURNISS

RAINTREE
STECK-VAUGHN
PUBLISHERS

A Harcourt Company

Austin   New York
www.steck-vaughn.com

Spinning through space
THE
MOON

Other titles in the series:

The Earth • The Sun • The Solar System

Cover photographs:
Lunar Prospector in orbit around the moon, 1998 [main];
astronaut Buzz Aldrin, 1969 [inset left]; *Saturn 5* spacecraft [inset middle];
crescent moon over California

Title page: Earthshine on the moon

Published by Raintree Steck-Vaughn Publishers, an imprint of Steck-Vaughn Company

Printed in Italy. Bound in the United States.
1 2 3 4 5 6 7 8 9 0 05 04 03 02 01

Library of Congress Cataloging-in-Publication Data
Furniss, Tim.
The moon / Tim Furniss.
   p.   cm.—(Spinning through space)
   Includes bibliographical references and index.
   Summary: Describes the composition, movements, eclipses, and exploration of the moon, as well as various theories about its formation.
   ISBN 0-7398-2738-3 (HC)
   0-7398-3090-2 (SC)
   1. Moon—Juvenile literature.
   [1. Moon.]
   I. Title. II. Series.
QB582.F87 2000
523.3—dc21   00-020759

CONTENTS

THE EARTH'S COMPANION

Most nights, we can look up and see the moon shining bright in the night sky. It always seems to be there. The moon is our constant companion. We look at the moon with a sense of wonder, just as the first humans did thousands of years ago.

▼ A full moon rising over a coastal cliff in Mexico

Except for the sun, the moon is the brightest object in the sky. Throughout each month, the moon appears to change shape. When the full moon is shining, it looks like a face. We call the face "the Man in the Moon."

It takes astronauts in a rocket three days to reach the moon. It would take 9,636 trillion days for a rocket to reach the edge of the known universe.

The moon orbits our Earth. It is just a small part of the solar system, a big family of nine planets and many moons that orbit our nearest star, the sun. The sun is just one of millions of stars in a huge galaxy that we call the Milky Way. There are millions of other galaxies like the Milky Way in the universe. The universe is huge, and the Earth, the moon, and the sun are only tiny parts of it.

▼ The nine planets that orbit the sun.

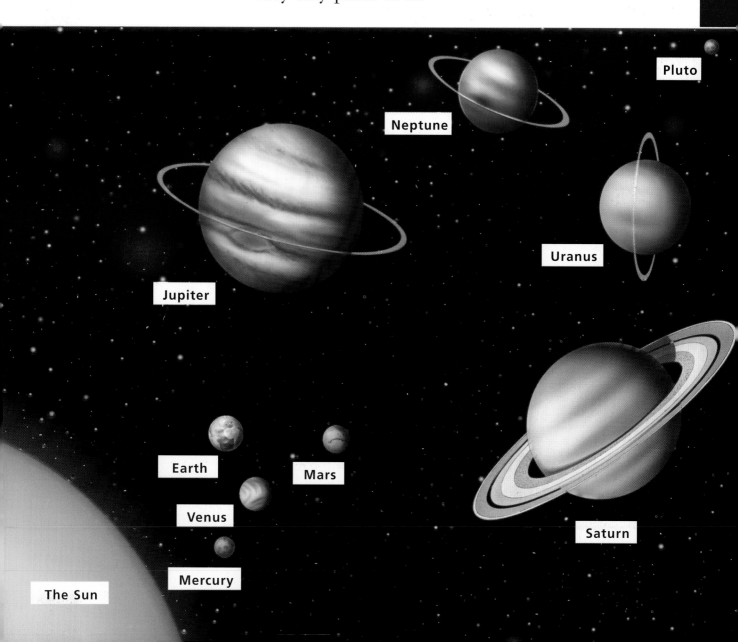

Pluto

Neptune

Uranus

Jupiter

Earth

Mars

Venus

Saturn

Mercury

The Sun

MOONS IN THE SOLAR SYSTEM

Many other planets in our solar system have moons. There are nine planets in the solar system: Mercury and Venus don't have moons; Earth has one moon; Mars, the red planet, has two; Jupiter, the largest planet, has more than 16 moons. Saturn, the ringed planet, has at least 17 moons; Uranus has 15; Neptune has six; and Pluto, the smallest and most distant planet, has one moon.

▼ The Martian moon, Phobos, rises in the west in the Mars sky and sets in the east four-and-a-half hours later.

There may be undiscovered moons orbiting these planets that are so small they have remained unseen by telescopes on Earth.

Io, a moon ▶ of Jupiter, has volcanoes that spew sulfur gas 174 mi. (280 km) out into space.

Not all moons are spherical like our moon. Many look like huge rocks. They may once have been planets or rocky asteroids that were captured by the gravity of a main planet when spinning through space. The gravity of the planets may have dragged the moons into orbit around them.

Billions of years ago, our moon may once have been a planet on its own. It now orbits the Earth.

The bright crescent of the moon is lit by sunlight, and the dimmer shade is lit by earthshine. ▶

MOON FACTS

The moon does not make any light of its own. The light we see is reflected sunlight. In reality, the moon has a very dark surface. Only about 7 percent of the sun's light is reflected by it. Sometimes, the moon is also lit by sunlight reflected off the Earth. This is called earthshine. When earthshine hits the moon, you see a bright crescent and a dimmer shade of the rest of the moon.

The gravity on the moon is one-sixth that of the Earth. The high jump world record is about 8.2 ft. (2.5 m). On the moon that would be 50 ft (15 m).

The moon is 2,378 mi. (3,746 km) in diameter. It orbits the Earth at a maximum distance of 247,674 mi. (398,581 km) at a speed of 2,287 mph (3,680 kph). The closest the moon comes to the Earth is 216,425 mi. (348,294 km). The moon takes 28 days, a lunar month, to orbit our planet once.

We only ever see one side of the moon because, as it is orbiting our Earth, it is also spinning around. It takes 28 days to spin once, the same time it takes to orbit the Earth. We cannot see the moon's far side, because it is always turned away from us. The temperature of the moon varies from 221° F (105° C) in the bright sunlight to minus 247° F (minus 155° C) in the shade.

The moon once orbited the Earth at a closer distance of 39,770 mi. (64,000 km). It is moving away from Earth in its orbit very slowly.

▼ The moon is about one-third the diameter of the Earth, although it looks a lot smaller in this photograph.

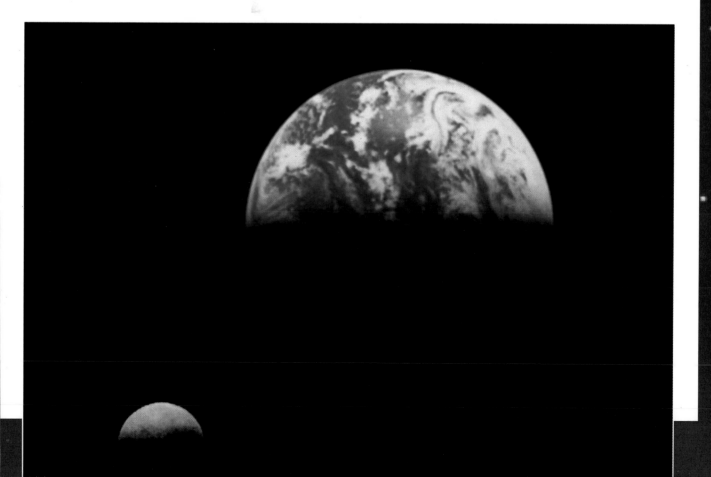

THE SURFACE OF THE MOON

When you look at the moon, you can see the famous "Man in the Moon" face. This is caused by the difference between the light and dark areas on the surface. The lighter areas are covered by craters and mountains. The darker areas, called mares, or seas, are large, smooth, flat plains that were mistaken for "seas" by early astronomers. This explains why the areas have names such as the Sea of Clouds and the Sea of Tranquillity.

The largest crater on the side of the moon that we can see is called Clavius. It is 144 mi. (232 km) in diameter.

◀ The moon's surface has many features, such as craters, deep valleys, high ridges, mountains, and smooth, dark areas called mares, or seas.

The moon's heated history

The moon's surface used to be very active early in its history. Meteorites and other rocks crashed down from space onto the moon and formed the many craters that we can see on its surface.

When meteorites crashed into the moon's surface forming craters, the material ejected from the surface formed lines called rays. The rays of the crater Tycho at the moon's south pole can be seen with the naked eye.

Later, lava oozed out of the moon's core and through the mantle. It spread across the surface, forming the smooth, dark areas we can see, called mares. At the same time, the soft lava was bombarded by more heavy meteorites and other bodies that hit the moon's surface while spinning through space. This created the moon's basins and craters. The moon's lunar mountains were also formed at about this time by the movement of lava.

◀ The moon's surface was heated and scarred by the impact of rocks crashing down from space.

Craters great and small

Many large craters were named after famous people, especially famous astronomers. One of the most famous craters is called Copernicus because it is large and very visible. The brightest crater is called Aristarchus. It has very light-colored dust that reflects light hitting the moon. The most spectacular craters are those with "rays." Rays are made of material that was ejected from the craters when they were formed by the impact of a meteorite.

▼ A valley called Hadley Rille is 84 mi. (135 km) long, 1,214 ft. (370 m) deep, and 1.2 mi. (2 km) wide. It was visited by the *Apollo 15* astronauts in 1971.

This diagram shows a cross-section of the moon from its core to outer crust. ▶

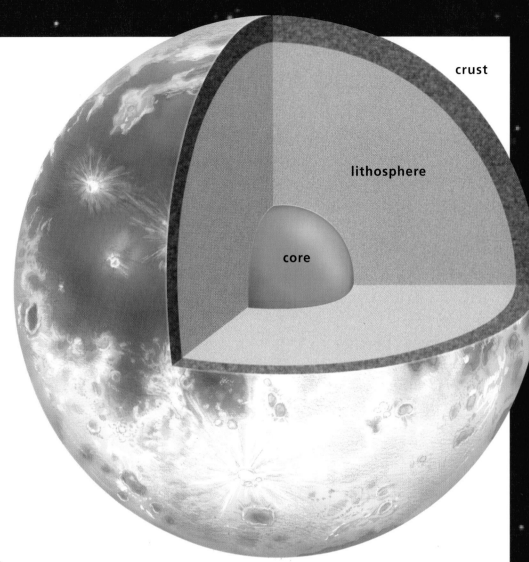

crust

lithosphere

core

Under the surface

The moon is a rocky body made up of several different layers. Its small central core is about 620 mi. (1,000 km) in diameter. This is covered by a layer of lunar mantle, about 373 mi. (600 km) thick, called the lithosphere. Finally, there is a 40-mi (65-km) thick layer of outer crust. Spacecraft have detected evidence that there may be water or ice beneath the surface. Ice has been found in very dark, cold areas around the moon's poles.

The moon's surface is the same as it was thousands of years ago, because there is no atmosphere or wind on the moon. In 1969, Neil Armstrong, the first astronaut on the moon, created footprints that will be there for thousands of years.

THE MOON'S MOVEMENT AND EARTH

The moon's movement around the Earth causes a reaction on the Earth's surface. It affects the Earth's atmosphere and its oceans.

If the Earth were one big ocean, the tidal bulge would travel once around the Earth in 24 hours and 50 minutes. That is the time of one moonrise to the next.

Tides

The ocean tides are caused by the moon's gravity. As the Earth spins, the pull of the moon's gravity causes the water to "bulge." On the side of the Earth that is away from the moon, the effect of the moon's gravity is less.

▼ A combination of different images made into one photo shows the Earth rising over the moon's surface.

tides

moon

moon

tides

sun

sun

The water moves away from the Earth and forms another slight bulge. In between the bulges, the water is low. It is a bit like a tug-of-war. The bulges are high tides, and the low water is the low tide. Sometimes the sun affects tides as well. When the moon is in line between the sun and the Earth, the sun's gravity pull is added to the moon's, making it stronger. This results in very high tides, called spring tides. Tides that stay at the same level are called neap tides.

▲ This artwork shows spring tide (left) and neap tide (right) bulges around the Earth.

The moon's gravity has slowed the speed of the Earth's rotation. Long ago, it was much faster and days were much shorter.

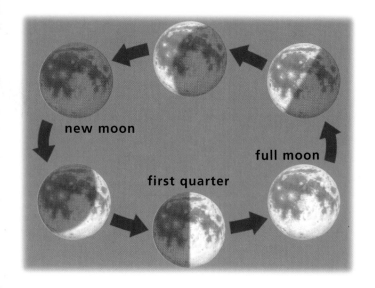

new moon

first quarter

full moon

▲ The phases of the moon go from new moon to full moon, then backward to new moon again.

Does the moon change shape?

The moon appears to change shape during its orbit around the Earth each month. These are called the phases of the moon. These phases are due to the way we see the moon as it changes position along its orbit.

A crescent moon over California ▶

The invisible moon

There is one phase of the moon that we cannot see. This occurs monthly when the moon is between the sun and Earth. Its far side is lighted up. The side of the moon that we normally see is lost in the dark night sky. This is called the new moon.

Changing times

The moon orbits the Earth in 28 days. It moves in the same direction that the Earth turns—to the east. The moon will rise in the east and set in the west. One day it may rise at 7:00 P.M. A day later, the Earth will have turned once. The moon then rises later and the next day, later still. This process continues. Sometimes, the moon can be seen during the day. The moon appears in the sky at different times each day.

▲ The moon never really changes shape. What we see depends on how much of the sunlit side is turned toward the Earth.

ECLIPSES

As the moon orbits the Earth and the Earth orbits the sun, the Earth and moon sometimes cross over each other's sunlight. This causes shadows called eclipses. There are two main types of eclipses: solar eclipses and lunar eclipses.

A few hundred years ago, natives of the West Indies sent food to the ship belonging to the famous explorer Christopher Columbus, when they were frightened by a lunar eclipse. They thought that Columbus had caused it by anchoring his ship off the island.

Solar eclipses

From the Earth, the moon seems to be almost the same size as the sun. The moon sometimes passes directly in front of the sun, causing a total solar eclipse. Sometimes, the moon causes only a partial eclipse when it does not block out all of the sun. There is a third kind of solar eclipse called an annular eclipse. This is when we can see the thin outer ring of the sun's disk, because the smaller disk of the moon does not cover it.

▼ The moon blots out all of the sun's disk causing a total solar eclipse.

During a total lunar eclipse, the moon looks red because the color of the sunsets and sunrises on the Earth reflects onto its dark surface. ▶

Lunar eclipses

Lunar eclipses occur when the Earth comes between the sun and the moon. The moon orbits the Earth at a slightly tipped angle. This sometimes causes the moon to pass into the shadow of the Earth. Once in a while, the moon passes through the shadow, causing a total eclipse that turns the moon a dramatic dark reddish-brown color. This light shines from the Earth to the moon's dark surface. Sometimes, only a part of the moon enters the shadow, causing a partial eclipse.

The brightness or dimness of the reddish-brown color of the moon during an eclipse depends on conditions in the Earth's atmosphere.

MOON EXPLORATION

In the past fifty years, technology has blasted into space. We have learned more about the moon from spacecraft than we ever did with telescopes on Earth.

The first spacecraft

The first spacecraft were launched in 1958, but they were not successful. Sometimes the rocket exploded, or the spacecraft fell back to Earth. Later, some craft hit the moon or flew past it, sending back basic science data. The Soviet *Luna 2* hit the moon in January 1959. The American *Pioneer 4* flew past the moon in 1959.

The far side of the moon remained hidden from humans for thousands of years. No eyes had seen it until the photos from *Luna 3* were transmitted to Earth in October 1959.

▼ This image of most of the far side of the moon was taken by *Lunar Orbiter*. The lines are caused by the separate scans the spacecraft made.

The far side of the moon

In October 1959, most of the far side of the moon was revealed for the first time. The Soviet *Luna 3* flew behind the moon, took photos, and transmitted them back to the Earth. It was a great moment in history. The images from *Luna 3* showed about 70 percent of the far side and some parts of the moon that we can see from Earth. The biggest surprise was that the far side seemed to be almost covered with craters and mountains. There seemed to be no smooth mares. The far side has many special features, such as the crater Tsiolkovsky and the Orientale Basin.

The first people to see the far side with their own eyes were the *Apollo 8* crew. They circled the moon for the first time in December 1968.

The moon's far side as seen by *Apollo 8* ▶

Further unmanned exploration

In January 1966, *Luna 9* landed on the moon and sent back the first images from its surface. It was followed by the American *Surveyor* spacecraft. *Surveyor 3* scooped up moondust with a shovel on the end of a robot arm in 1967. *Luna 10* became the first spacecraft to orbit the moon in 1966. American *Lunar Orbiters* mapped the moon's surface in 1966–67. They sent back spectacular images of almost the whole of the moon's surface.

The U.S. *Lunar Prospector* spacecraft may have found water or ice under the soil of the moon's poles. *Lunar Prospector* was launched in January 1998. ▶

An *Apollo 16* astronaut, Charlie Duke, worked on the moon's surface with the help of the *Lunar Rover.* ▶

The Apollo moonwalkers

Among the most exciting events in the history of the twentieth century were the explorations of the moon by the first humans in 1969–72. The astronauts were called the *Apollo* moonwalkers. There were six landings on the moon. Twelve people walked on it in various areas, from the smooth Sea of Tranquillity to the highlands of Taurus Littrow.

Pieces of *Surveyor 3*, which soft-landed on the moon in 1967, were brought back to Earth by the *Apollo 12* astronauts in 1969.

The moon landings allowed scientists on Earth to find out more about the moon's surface. The moonwalkers brought back moon rocks to be analyzed. They also left many scientific tools on the surface to send information back to Earth.

On July 20, 1969, *Apollo 11* made the first manned landing. Neil Armstrong and Buzz Aldrin were the first men on the moon. *Apollo 12*'s Pete Conrad and Al Bean followed in November 1969. *Apollo 13* did not make a landing. *Apollo 14* landed in February 1971. The moonwalkers were Alan Shepard and Edgar Mitchell. A Lunar Roving Vehicle was driven across the moon's surface by *Apollo 15* astronauts David Scott and Jim Irwin in July 1971. *Apollo 16* landed in April 1972 with John Young and Charlie Duke aboard.

The last men on the moon were Gene Cernan and Jack Schmitt in December 1972. No humans have been to the moon since then.

▲ Buzz Aldrin stands in the lunar dust in this photo taken by Neil Armstrong.

The six *Apollo* crews came back to Earth with a total of 850 lb. (385 kg) of the moon.

The rush to the moon

The flight of *Apollo 11* was the very first time that humans had left their home planet and landed on another world. It was a truly historic moment in our history. But the *Apollo* program was an expensive one, and when the money ran out, the program ended. Probably the greatest spin-off from *Apollo* was the view of the tiny Earth as seen from space. Suddenly, the world seemed a lot smaller and lost in the vast universe.

Neil Armstrong's first words when he stepped on the moon were, "That's one small step for man, one giant leap for mankind."

▼ Geologist astronaut Jack Schmitt of *Apollo 17* took samples of the moon's surface to examine.

OBSERVING THE MOON

It is easy to observe the moon. By just using your eyes, you can make out the mare or "sea" areas. You can even see some of the bright features, such as the rays coming from the crater Tycho during a full moon.

Through a pair of binoculars, the scene is transformed to a fantastic sight. You can see many craters and even the mountains. They are best seen during the phases of the moon rather than the full moon.

Larger telescopes have motors on them so that they can match the moon's speed and follow it as it moves across the sky.

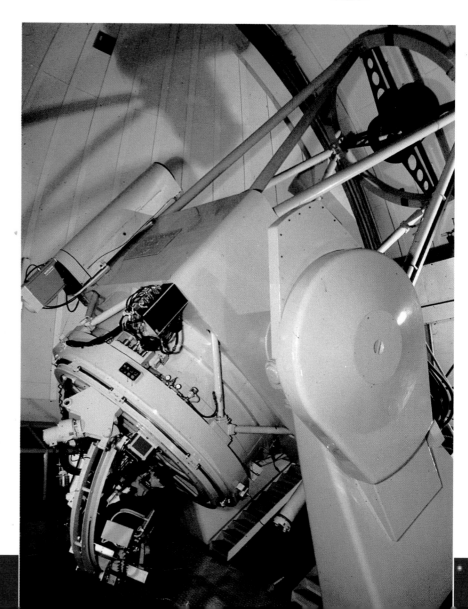

Powerful telescopes with motors such as this one are kept in observatories. ▶

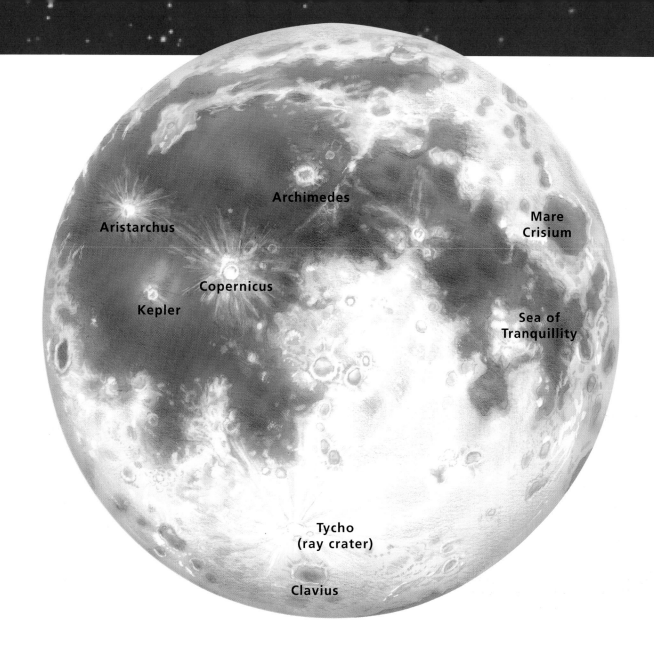

Archimedes

Aristarchus

Mare Crisium

Copernicus

Kepler

Sea of Tranquillity

Tycho (ray crater)

Clavius

A small telescope can show even greater detail. If you hold the telescope in your hands, it might be difficult to keep still. Place the telescope on a stand or a tripod to help you. However, the moon never stays still, and its movement across the sky can seem to be faster when looking through a telescope. You will need to move the telescope slightly sideways to keep up.

▲ A map of the moon. The Mare Crisium, top right, is the Man in the Moon's left ear.

The first map of the moon to be drawn using observations through a telescope was made in July 1609 by Thomas Harriot of England.

NOTES FOR TEACHERS

The Earth's Companion

Ask pupils to make a diary of the time and days they see the moon, what time it rose or set, and what its phase was. Ask them to draw the phases as they see them.

Moons in the Solar System

Demonstrate the movement of the Earth and the moon as they orbit the sun. Stand a pupil, the "sun," in the middle of a large room. Get two people to stand some feet away. Let one, "the Earth," walk slowly around the "sun" in a circle counterlockwise. The other should walk around the "Earth" while at the same time walking around the "sun." Have the "moon" walk in a spiral movement, while the "Earth" moves slowly within the spiral.

Moon Facts

Put a ball on the end of string and whirl the string around to simulate an "orbit." Observe how the speed keeps the ball at the end of the string.

The Surface of the Moon

Show how craters are made by making a "mud pie" mixture on a tray and dropping stones onto it.

The Moon's Movement and Earth

• Explain gravity as the force of two objects against each other.

• Demonstrate how the phases work by using a flashlight (sunlight) and a large ball (the moon) in a dark room. Place the ball in front of the pupils. Ask one pupil to move the flashlight around the room shining it at the ball, while the others stay in the same place watching the ball. They will see the moon go from a full moon when the sunlight is in front of the moon to a crescent shape when the sunlight is just behind the moon.

Eclipses

Demonstrate how an object eclipses another by moving across it, using a light and a ball. Show how you can create the effect of a lunar eclipse using a light and two balls.

Moon Exploration

Find newspaper articles from 1969, and imagine the excitement of exploring the moon. Ask the pupils to write a magazine article as if they were the first people to explore the moon.

Observing the Moon

One evening, observe the moon. Locate the "seas" and name them. See if you can pick out Tycho and a few other of the brighter craters. Use a pair of binoculars to observe closer. Use the map on page 27 as a guide.

GLOSSARY

Asteroids Bodies of rock that orbit the sun.

Astronauts A person who travels through space in a spacecraft.

Astronomers People who study the stars.

Atmosphere The air around the Earth.

Basins A wide, rounded dip in a surface.

Core The central part of something.

Craters Deep, wide holes on a surface.

Crescent A narrow curve; the moon is crescent-shaped in two of its phases.

Diameter The length drawn between one side of a circle or sphere to the opposite side through its center.

Galaxy A mass of millions of stars in the sky.

Gravity A pulling force that brings objects closer to a large object, such as a planet.

Lava Melted rock that has surfaced from the core of a planet.

Lunar Having something to do with the moon.

Mantle The inner layer of a moon or planet that lies between the core and the surface.

Meteorites Rocks that float through space, occasionally drawn by gravity to the surface of a large object such as a planet.

Optical illusion Something that appears different from what it really is.

Orbit To go around.

Phases Stages of change, such as the different shapes of the moon that we can see from Earth.

Solar system The sun and the nine planets that orbit it and their moons.

Spherical Round all over, like a ball.

FURTHER INFORMATION

Websites:
www.fourmilab.ch/earthview/vplanet.html
Earth and Moon Viewer
You can view the moon from this website
and find up-to-date information on its
different phases.

www.nasa.gov/
This is NASA's homepage
which contains pictures and information
about ongoing space exploration.

Places to visit:
National Air and Space Museum
7th and Independence Ave., S.W.
Washington, D.C. 20560
(202) 357-2700
www.nasm.edu

NASA/Kennedy Space Center
Kennedy Space Center, FL 32899
(407) 452-2121
www.ksc.nasa.gov

BOOKS TO READ

Books to read:

Gibbons, Gail. *The Moon Book*.
  Holiday House, 1997.

Graham, Dan. *The Best Book of the
  Moon*. Larousse Kingfisher
  Chambers, 1999.

Vogt, Gregory. *Earth*. Millbrook, 1996.

Walker, Niki. *The Moon*. Crabtree,
  1998.

Picture acknowledgments:

The publishers would like to thank the following for allowing us to reproduce their pictures in this book: Bruce Coleman Ltd./Dr Scott Nielsen 17; Eye Ubiquitous/NASA 2, 10, 18, 25; Genesis Photo Library *cover*, 6, 7, 9, 12, 20, 21, 22, /NASA *cover*, 12, 23; Science Photo Library 11, /David Nanuk 2, 4, /Royal Greenwich Observatory 26, /John Sanford *title page*, 8, /Frank Zullo *cover*, 3, 16, 19; The Stock Market/NASA 14.

The illustrations on pages 5, 13, 15, 16 and 27 are by Peter Bull.

INDEX

All numbers in **bold** refer to pictures as well as text.